A Man and A Horse

A Man
and
A Horse

Poems by

Arnie Johanson

Ortenstone Press
Durham, NC

ACKNOWLEDGMENTS

The author wishes to thank the editors of the following publications in which these poems (or earlier versions of them) originally appeared:
    Light, "How Now! A Rat?"
    Main Street Rag, "Injury Ousts Buddha"
    Pinesong (North Carolina Poetry Society),
      "Ancient Greek Wisdom," "The Good Citizen"
    Red Weather, "Squeezed," "Epic Hope"
    Simul, "Reformation"
    DILR Newsletter, "Horse-manship"

Special thanks to my mentors: Florence Nash, Douglas Goetsch, and Linda Back McKay

Copyright © 2007   Arnie Johanson
All rights reserved

ISBN 978-0-6151-8173-8

For Alice,

who makes everything possible

Contents

Apology *Pro Vita Mea*	1
The Philosophical Life	2
Ancient Greek Wisdom	3
Scruples	4
Welcome to America	5
The Good Citizen	7
"We Don't Bother With Rhyme and Meter Anymore"	8
"How Now! A Rat?"	9
Injury Ousts Buddha	11
Reformation	13
Rida, Rida, Ranka	14
Christmas Eves With Grandma	15
Olivia's Recital	17
Awful Things	18
Trouble With a Capital P	19
The Course of True Love	20
How To Love a Stranger	23

Will You Still Need Me?	24
Well-tempered in Leipzig	25
Pete Seeger, Summer of 2001	26
Imagine	27
Heavens, It Was Tasty	28
Horse-manship	29
Building a Man	30
To the Face in the Mirror, After Thirty Days of Shaving, After Thirty Years Unshaven	31
Squeezed	32
Epic Hope	33
Missing My Muse	34

He . . . flung himself upon his horse, and rode madly off in all directions.

Stephen Leacock

Apology *Pro Vita Mea*

I would have been a great philosopher.
Not Plato, Kant, or Wittgenstein, of course,
but known to every *au courant* professor,
the subject of symposia, the source
of streams of abstruse discourse, widely cited.
But I found the dreary toil required to gather
scholarly encomiums invited
desolation and divorce. So, rather

than write treatises for journals, whose
editors know wisdom if and only if
it bites them in the balls, those jerks who choose
to print pure shit (not mine), I vowed to shift
my energies to educating youth
who yearn to learn of right and wrong and beauty
and nineteen ways to parse the concept *truth*.
I heard their call, pursued my teaching duty

tormented by an endless flow of deans'
administrivia, and my wife
and kids, who needed gadgetry and jeans.
All that explains my unproductive life.
That, plus sudoku, crosswords, junk TV,
computer games, old movie DVDs,
piano, banjo, guitar errantry . . .
I'm reduced to beer and tattered BVDs.

So if someday you chance to drop my name
to a philosopher, she'll say "don't know it."
But that's OK. I've given up that game.
From here on out I'm going to be a poet.

The Philosophical Life

Frustrated Socrates paces the agora
from stall to stall. What was it
Xanthippe warned him
not to dare come home without?
Eggplant? olives? leg of lamb?
Is it even possible, he wonders,
to remember things forgotten.
If something, say an eggplant,
is truly gone from memory,
then even if you think "eggplant"
you won't remember it's eggplant you forgot.

Why, he wonders, does she get
upset when I forget.
I've shown her many times
that no one can forget on purpose.
To forget an eggplant, say, on purpose
you'd have to remember it's an eggplant
you are trying to forget.

So many questions. If only he could
find a few young men to talk things over.
But the boys are all avoiding him,
what with that trial coming up.
The trial doesn't worry him.
A jury can be reasoned with.
But Xanthippe! Why, he wonders,
do wives have to be women?

And where does Virtue lead him now?
Bring nothing home and face full wifely wrath?
Or bring a chicken, or an eggplant,
anything to show her he remembered
there was *something* that she wanted?
And if by chance he gets it right
will it be wrong to take the credit?
He wanders home, still wondering.

Ancient Greek Wisdom

You can't be sure you're happy till you're dead;
there's so much could go wrong while you're still here.
So Solon, Aeschylus and others said.

The Dow could plunge and leave you bathed in red,
out on the street without a sou for beer.
You can't be sure you're happy till you're dead.

You come home early, find your wife in bed,
commingled with some smarmy sonneteer.
Her smile reminds you what some wise Greeks said.

Your grandkids that you love so much all wed
mafiosi or Republicans. It's clear
you can't be sure you're happy till you're dead.

Some weird psychosis, latent in your head,
bursts into bloom. Greek voices you now hear
taunt "We were right in everything we said."

Alzheimer's, cancer, AIDS, some fate you dread
brings pain and angst that will not disappear.
You can't be sure you're happy till you're dead.
So Solon, Aeschylus and I have said.

Scruples

At each semester's end they came,
young men who knew the grade they'd earned
would make their draft deferment history.
They'd plead with me to raise the grade to C
to guarantee their coming back
next term. I always told them "No.
If you had only come to class
once in a while, or read the text,
or turned your papers in on time,
maybe then I could accommodate you.
But there's no way in hell that I can give
you any more than you deserve."
Do I deserve to go to Vietnam?
they'd ask. My only answer,
"That isn't up to me."

Most often I would see them back
on campus the next term. But one,
at least, wound up in Vietnam.
That's his name inscribed here
on the Wall.

Welcome to America

Henriquez calls. His quaking voice
spits out two words of frantic English:
Go . . . bank.

At his apartment, trembling,
he hands me a letter,
his first piece of U. S. mail.
It's from Ed McMahon.
The envelope boldly proclaims
that he, Henriquez S.,
has won one million dollars.

A year on the run in Haiti,
hiding from militia who raped
and murdered his wife,
he's been here just one week.
Without mother and sister
he spends days and nights
learning women's work,
how to cook, keep house,
care for two small girls.

The open dictionary on the desk,
the Creole scrawls on notebook pages,
reveal his struggle to decipher
the envelope's message.
The gleam in his eyes and crack
in his voice prove his success.
Fantasies about America realized,
he will be a real man again.

I don't know French or Creole
for *junk mail, fine print, scam.*
All I can do is hold the envelope,
point at its boldfaced lie,

shake my head, repeat
some English words he knows:
No . . . no . . . bullshit . . . no . . .

The fire in his eyes dies.

The Good Citizen

I hear the screams. I do not care to look.
It sounds like it's a woman being raped.
I hide inside the pages of my book
and wish the windows were more thickly draped.

It sounds just like a woman being raped.
I know I should at least take one small glance
outside, through windows not-so-thickly draped,
to see what's going on. There is a chance

I'll see, if I should take that one small glance,
some teens at play, or crazy Mrs. Brown
and her weird goings-on. Maybe. Fat chance!
Whoever's screaming needs help soon. That sound's

not playful teens, or dotty Doris Brown.
I should go beat the bastard off of her.
That screaming woman needs help now. It sounds
like hero-time for me. But I'll defer.

I'm old. I can't beat bastards off of her.
And it might be a gang. I could get killed.
Dead hero? Not for me. I'll just defer.
Conscience pangs are better than death's chill.

If it's a gang, one dead's enough. I'll kill
my guilt by hiding out inside my book.
The pains of conscience beat death's endless chill.
Silence. I still hear her screams. Too late to look.

"We Don't Bother With Rhyme and Meter Anymore"
A Voice at Every Workshop I Attend

They speak for modern poetry, I guess,
and random reading seems to bear them out.
But every line I write, to their distress,
is iamb after iamb, and no doubt
my poems evoke a *sotto voce* curse
when I insist on rhyme in every verse.

You can't let line breaks happen willy-nilly
or all you have is convoluted prose.
Arrhythmic poems? dispassionate and chilly.
God help me! there I go again! who knows

if there's a cure for hopeless rhyme addiction?
"Hello, I'm Arnie. I'm iamboholic."
Some pal to call each time my mad affliction
moves hand toward pen. Or is it diabolic?

A priest with chants and cross could exorcise me,
expel those demons I once thought were muses.
If all else fails, let them lobotomize me.
Free verse might flow from surgical abuses.

Addictions can't be cured, of course. I know
my demon-muses will not be destroyed
by any force on earth, above, below.
So I follow where they lead me, unannoyed
by vagaries of taste, aesthetic fashion
and pompous asses dissing metric passion.

"How Now! A Rat?"
Hamlet, Act III, Scene iv

Young Abelard, fat laboratory rat,
smashed all experimental expectations,
learned colors, sounds and shapes, pressed levers that
provided gourmet food and sweet libations.

He learned the lever marked with XXX
would earn him time with rat-babe Heloise.
He soon grew bored with food and drink and sex,
thought writing poetry might help him ease

his distraught mind. Whatever it might cost,
he swore he'd prove an ordinary rat
could out-write Shakespeare, Dickinson and Frost.
He learned the alphabet in no time flat.

The keyboard proved, for Abelard, no sweat.
He slimmed down as he leapt across the keys.
His rat tail worked the mouse, his dexterous set
of paws punched out a poem sure to please

the most fastidious editor. He'd win
a Pulitzer, he thought; but heartache lurked.
Those "Thank you, but . . ." type notices poured in.
He'd send new poems out, but nothing worked.

You see, the rat wrote formal poetry.
Petrarchan sonnets, villanelles, and odes
Pindaric, ghazals, rondelays, rubai,
he tried them all, tried many other modes.

His cage was littered with rejection slips.
His muse deserted him, and, even worse,
he started smoking pot, took acid trips.
On one such trip he tried to write free verse.

It made no sense to him, no rhyme or meter,
but still he sent it out, by force of habit.
He sent his trainer out to get a liter
of vintage Ratschild Chateauneuf-du-Pape. It

brought a six-week high. A note came saying "Cheers!
That poem you sent us really was a corker.
We're pleased to tell you it will soon appear
next to a cat cartoon in *The New Yorker*."

So if *New Yorker* poetry puzzles you
and makes you ask "Just what the hell is that?"
Those words that seem misplaced, obscure, askew,
might come from Abelard, a spaced-out rat.

Injury Ousts Buddha
Raleigh *News and Observer,* May 4, 2002

Buddha sprained his foot
and was scratched
from the Kentucky Derby.
Damn!
I didn't know *he'd* entered.

I see and hear what might have been:
"In gate #4,
from Nirvana Stables
wearing saffron,
jockeying himself . . ."

The gates spring open
launching the horses –
and Buddha.
As the dust clears we see Buddha
strolling calmly,
far behind.

Heading down the homestretch
Buddha appears
out of Nothingness,
ahead of the pack.
He crosses the line,
bowing politely.

They try to hang a garland
round his neck.
He insists it be dismantled
so that everyone can have a flower.

For the media, he explains
that there really is no difference
between victory and defeat,

or a man and a horse.
Rose in hand
he moves on down the track.

Reformation

My friends all wanted to be Superman
when they grew up. I wanted to be Martin Luther,
a fortress for the Lord, standing strong
against the Pope and all his wicked priests.
I'd slay them with the truth. I'd shout God's Word,
rescuing Rome's victims from the mouth of hell.
I'd take on Lucifer himself, like Luther did,
but my ink wouldn't miss its mark.

I did stand up before the Pope one day, stared
squarely in his eyes through my Kodak Pony.
He looked like Uncle Frank, chubby, gray,
a smile that nobody could ever want to fight.
I shared good Lutheran beer with priests I met.
They did not try to trick me into deeding
my possessions and posterity to the Holy See.
I never found the monsters Mother warned me of.

I could still do battle with the devil, I suppose.
He's never shown himself to me in any form
that I could throw things at. He may have been
a partner in some projects I pursued. It's hard
to fight an enemy who lurks inside your skin,
especially when you kinda like the lurking.
And the sword of truth is useless when its edge
gets blunted by confusion and despair.

I never will be Luther. But my friends
can't even leap doghouses in single bounds.
We go on being who we are. God help us.

Rida, Rida, Ranka

As she bounced me on her knee she sang a song
about a boy who rides a wooden horse.
He longs to be a knight, fight hard, grow strong
but love and marriage knock him off his course.
She'd segue to an ancient Swedish hymn
whose gentler rhythm rocked me in her arms,
safe and secure, as children are with Him
who keeps us all from any lasting harm.
I couldn't understand a single word,
the moral lessons blew straight through my ears.
But the rhythm's in my bones, and I've not heard
or sung that hymn without a tear for years.
The messages have mingled. Now I see
the love of God's a bounce on Grandma's knee.

Christmas Eves With Grandma

1949

I ripped the paper off the box and stared.
A record player? The tag said it was mine
but she must have meant this treasure to be shared.
She usually sent a shirt. A gift this fine
was well beyond her means. A closer look
confirmed it was for me, without mistake:
three children's albums, one with Disney book,
and, coiled around the spindle – a green snake.

The snake was five and dime variety.
Each year she sent me one, deployed with care
to burst forth unexpectedly and scare
me just a bit, fear soon transformed to glee.
In months the phonograph was obsolete.
One snake survives; my favorite Christmas treat.

1975

Mortician arts have almost made you look
just like you did some twenty years ago.
Up on the wall, the Shepherd with his crook
invites you home. Your family left below
has gathered on the morn of Christmas Eve
to hail a life lived with uncommon flair.
I'm overcome by floods of memory
as our Swedish hymn is sung.
                    We say a prayer
commending you to Him who tends the flock.

I think, as you are laid into the earth,
I should have slipped a snake inside your box
so you could startle God at your new birth.
You'll have five drops with Him when you awake.
Goodbye, and thanks for coffee, songs and snakes.

Olivia's Recital

She glows more brightly than the tree, which stands
watch next to her, intent, as are we all,
on hearing every word as she enthralls
with ancient carols from her native land.
This show goes on each year, at our demand.
She always says *Nej, nej! I don't recall
the words, I'm not prepared.* Her ritual
reluctance is ignored. We understand.
We know that she's been practicing for weeks,
her costume chosen and prepared with care.
She holds a glass of red *vin ordinaire*,
her bit of sunshine on a frigid night.
We sing, off-key, can't get the Swedish right,
but in full harmony with her mystique.

Awful Things

My mother, proud life member
of the WCTU,
went on and on
about the "awful things"
liquor does to people.
She wouldn't tell me
why so many folks
enjoyed drinking stuff
that did such awful things.

At Kenny's house one day
I spied some whiskey in the fridge.
He got some glasses,
poured us each a healthy shot.
I drank mine straight down
like cowboys in movie saloons.
Nothing whiskey did
could have been as awful
as that taste, and the after-taste
that would not wash away.
Why anyone drank whiskey
when they could have pop
or Kool-Aid, still a mystery.

I never touched another drop
until I got to college.
Friends there assured me
it really does taste good
if you just drink it properly.
They proved their point
with a pint of Old Crow.
Anything but awful,
the things it did to me.

Trouble With a Capital P

The pool hall beckoned with flickering
fluorescents and walls of neon selling sin:
Hamm's, Grain Belt, Pabst Blue Ribbon.
Jerry Lee and Elvis rocked the juke box
to syncopated pool ball clicks. Cigarette
smoke blended with beer and a hint of vomit
to impart a scent to shirt and skin
impervious to Listerine and Sen-Sen.

When she caught a whiff of where I'd been
Mom reminded me, each time, that I was
never to set foot again inside that place
where heathen men hang out to smoke and drink,
tell dirty jokes and do all kinds of awful things
with pool hall Jezebels, those *loose* women.
I wasn't sure exactly what *loose* meant.
I knew where I would have to go to learn,
but billiard parlor women, tight or loose,
have no time for pimply boys.

Two girls my age showed up one day.
The pool hall loosened Linda's mouth,
as well as the top buttons of her blouse.
Melanie had a body more mature than she was.
Cracking jokes about cues and balls, the girls
whipped me at rotation, then suggested I go
with them to an abandoned house nearby.
I went, praying that Melanie
was as loose as rumor had it.

The Course of True Love

1. Dear Wine,

I didn't like you very much
when we met back in college.
We went to lots of the same parties
but I never felt an urge to bring you home.
Then working, married with a couple kids,
I found that you could brighten up a meal
in your Gallo Hearty Burgundy jug.
You came along to weekly Scrabble games
with the couple across the street. The women
ignored you, but you'd still be shot
when we got home. No longer just good friends,
the thing between us kept growing until

now I can't imagine life without you.
I love your exotic costumes
with designer labels. I'm jealous
of your fluency in romance languages.
Still, your discount outfits usually suit me fine,
so you don't yet cost me more than I can bear.
I admit I flirt with your hardass relatives,
and if you only serve me once at dinner,
I take it as permission to entertain
your sassy Scottish cousin before bed.
I hear you'll help me live a little longer
if we just visit for a bit each day.
It's so amazing what true love will do.

Please don't worry. This letter's
not a prelude to farewell. What you did
to my grandfathers? Long ago forgiven.
I simply thought it would be good
if we both knew how much I love you.

I'm sure you know I'm

Yours forever

2. *Dear Wine,*

Our torrid affair is over.

If I could only lie, and say
"I'm sorry dear, I just don't love you
anymore" or "I've found somebody else,"
this letter would be so much easier.

It isn't my idea. And not my wife's.
She's known about us all along.
My love for you never cooled
my love for her, so she's been cool with us.
It's that gang of medical professionals.
They think that our relationship
is harmful to my health, or even worse.
Headaches, heartaches, loss of sleep
are the normal price for love, of course.
But the price has soared beyond
what my poor body can afford.

As I sip insipid H_2O at dinner,
I'll be thinking of the tingles
when you caressed my nose,
and the swirl of your body
as it rolled across my tongue.
With my iced tea and Diet Coke
I'll be pining for your Pinots,
and I will savor our Riesling romps
and Merlot merriment forever.

We will still see each other

at receptions and soirées.
I'll be the guy with the decaf.
Perhaps we might do lunch sometime.
I'm only human, as you well know,
and humans sometimes cheat, so maybe . . . .
but it would never be the same.

From a distance, I remain

Yours forever

How To Love a Stranger

Just pick somebody. Anyone will do,
but these days I prefer a woman
who's mature, who's lived a bit
and isn't bothered by the fact.

I might find her at an airport gate,
sitting, waiting to depart.
It's better she be short than tall,
brunette (well-mixed with gray).
No designer clothes, just *Land's End* casual.
She's reading something serious
or working crossword puzzles,
drinking real coffee, black, grande.
A copy of the *Times* is in her purse.
That's a woman I could love.

I will not talk to her, of course.
This affair must play out in my mind.
I'll have her come to me.
Perhaps she'll see I'm writing, ask
"Are you a poet?" *Well, I try*
I say in my most charming way.
"Is it true that poets are great lovers?"
I can't speak for the others I reply.
I'm more than satisfied with me.
Why do you ask? I ask, in Bogart voice.
Her Bacall reply: "When we land,
we'll find a room, order some martinis,
and you will read me your poetry."

She walks by to board the plane.
I won't see her again, but I'll love her
until *I* decide it's over.
It's not that hard to love a stranger,
especially when she's so much like my wife.

Will You Still Need Me?
Paul McCartney

I needed you when we were younger.
You fed me, held my hand
(and other parts), and kept me sane
through grad school, children
and financial woes. I never knew
what I did for you, but had no doubt
you also needed me.

Some fifty years ago, if Ken and I
hadn't spent the night at your place,
playing cards with your roommates,
I never would have seen how cute you were
in your pajamas in the morning.
We would have each gone on alone
and found somebody else for mutual need.

Now, 64's a memory. When I go
you'll find others for Scrabble,
travel, concerts, Bulls games.
You'll get a cat to keep you warm.
And, God forbid, if you go first
I'll have to learn to do the laundry,
clean the house. But I'll get by.
The sad truth is: we do not need each other.

That's the fact. I know it well
but I still believe I need you.
And I have a hunch you think
you need me too. That's love's
sweet miracle of self-deception,
and love is all we really need.

Well-tempered in Leipzig

Did you ever rest, Johann Sebastian?
Constantly composing, desperate to meet
the Kapellmeister cantata quota.
Writing them, I'm sure, was easier
than teaching them to choirs
of adolescent prima donnas.

Did Anna Magdalena ever yell
as you headed out the door "Johann, wait!
Why not stay home this once?
Let them rehearse themselves.
We'll play a little gin, maybe drink
a little gin, then read some poetry."
When you dragged yourself home
from a long day in the loft,
did she help you out of your boots,
set you in the comfy chair,
gently rub your tender feet,
pour you a tall cold one or two,
hand you the *Zeitung*,
and keep the kids away until dinner?

All those kids! They show us
you and Anna were not content
with well-earned rest in bed.
Tell me, were there preludes
with your nocturnal fugues?
I did read somewhere once, I think,
that when at last you fell asleep
you snored in E-flat minor.

Pete Seeger, Summer of 2001

Pete picks a few bars
on that special long neck banjo,
lifts back his head, puffs out his chest,
looks toward the sky and belts out a song:
Let the midnight special shine its light on me.
A gesture ignites two hundred voices
in seeming perfect harmony.

Linked together, we sway to left and right
and sing that song we sang so often
way back when: *We Shall Overcome.*
We sing for all the great ideals:
Black and white together . . .
We shall live in peace . . .
We shall all be free . . .
Some . . . day."

Someday's been so slow to come.
Yet we keep singing
as if we really expect it.
Pete's face and posture tell me
he's never stopped believing
that if we all just sing together
we *shall* overcome.
As we sing and sway
I too believe.

Back home a few days later
some Carolina wrens hop
on the railing of our deck.
One of them lifts back its head,
puffs out its chest, looks toward the sky
and belts out a song.
Someday must be coming soon.

Imagine

I found Foster's Finest Formal Wear
in the bowels of one of the Dales.
My tux a perfect fit, they had no size eight shoes.
I'd have to go too big or too tight
for ten or twelve hours. An easy choice.
So there I was, my daughter on my arm,
my shoes stuffed with toilet paper, mincing
down the aisle trying to look normal
as I fought to keep my dogs inside their pens.
I slipped them off under the table at dinner,
confident chicken and prime rib aromas
would mask the odor. The first dance,
featuring bride and dad, loomed, making
the meal tasteless, the wine impotent.

The music started. John Lennon's *Imagine*.
Shoes back on, tissue redistributed, I took
the floor with Sara, feeling a spotlight on my feet.
No stepping, high or fancy. I just pushed to the music
and prayed. *Imagine . . . no hell below us . . .*
not hard to do when hell's right here.
Imagine . . . all the people . . . staring at my feet.
All I could imagine was a shoeless body
fallen on its face. *I hope someday you'll join us . . .*
Yes, yes. Isn't everyone supposed
to flood the dance floor after the first chorus?

Mercifully, the music stopped. Feet still shod,
I shuffled to the table to sit and think,
about marriages and shoes. No matter
how carefully you plan or how much you spend,
some things will never fit quite right.
You may think I'm a dreamer, but I believe
if you keep the tissue handy
and make a few adjustments,
with a bit of luck you'll be *living life in peace.*

Heavens, It Was Tasty
for Mark and Carolyn

In the backyard of an architectural oddball
in St. Paul, friends and family mingle
under an umbrella of American Elms
in a lake of ten thousand hostas,
with petunias in every shade of purple.
Beneath a large fruitless pear tree
a Powdermilk Biscuit Bandman's
folk guitar and vocals keep the mood mellow:
Shenandoah, Cripple Creek, Soldier's Joy,
Whiskey Before Breakfast.

Carolyn appears in a billowing sari
matching the petunia hues. Her daughter
Zoë strews pink and white rose petals
along the path, then matures to Maid of Honor.
Son Tyler, in tux-induced distress,
smiles bravely as Mark's best man.

       Introduced by the personal ads,
       they first met at the Stone Arch Bridge.
       Dinner by the river, then hours
       in the parking lot talking of their love
       for Eliot and J. Alfred Prufrock.

The ceremony is poetry and song.
Mark reads from *Prufrock*,
they improvise their vows,
the judge declares them wed.
We wind our way to the Mississippi
for a dinner cruise through the locks.
Under the Stone Arch Bridge, Zoë
tosses Mom's bouquet into the river
as the evening spreads out against the sky.

Horse-manship

He comes to me with smile and arms spread wide.
    I hoist him to my shoulders, gently place
        his strong young legs around my aging neck.

My hands and arms clasped firmly on his shins
    I start my slow exaggerated trot,
        the highlight of our horse and cowboy game.

He doesn't know what cowboys are, as yet,
    or even horses. Large four-legged beasts
        for him are all varieties of *moo*.

I tell him his old nag must stop to rest.
    He stays in saddle as we sit. He squeals,
        then kicks to spur me back into my trot.

I feel warm moisture trickle on my neck.
    I'm oddly unannoyed. I realize
        a neck wash for a horse is no big deal.

It's nothing but spontaneous overflow
    of joy in being big and riding tall,
        a situation gladly left unchanged.

Building a Man

Oskar calls: *Big Grandpa, help.*
The snowball he is rolling refuses
to grow more than softball size.
I'd rather play in anthrax than in snow,
but there's no way to say "no"
to a four-year-old's demand.
I agree to show him how it's done.

I build your standard snowman,
three balls high. I pack more snow
to seal his joints, arm him
with chokeberry branches,
press berries into place as
beady blood-shot eyes
to complement his broad beer-belly.
My wife, *Little Grandpa*, finds
a baby carrot for his nose,
a flowerpot to top him off.

I look for Oskar, find him busy
rolling a ball almost as tall
as he is. He strains to get his man-base
set next to my jolly inebriate,
then runs off to chase his sister.
I'm sure he plans to finish it someday.
He'll learn someday how
snowman days are numbered.

To the Face in the Mirror, After Thirty Days of Shaving, After Thirty Years Unshaven

Lathered up each morning
my disposable twin-blade Gillette glides
down cheeks and chin, across the upper lip,

and there you are again. It used to be
when I gazed into the glass
I always found *me* looking back.

But you, you're just some fucking stranger.
Not as ugly as I thought you'd be. Not quite.
Those cheeks, as sleek as what's on top

make you look some ten years younger.
What have you done with me?
Am I stashed inside an old Viagra vial

behind you? Forever smashed in some
Wonderland saloon? Or squeezed between
your glassy face and silvered ass?

Below the chin you do still look like me.
Same eighteen-plus red neck, absent biceps,
abundant abdomen, and down below,

where rejuvenation would be welcome,
no change. None of that stuff matters.
No body's any good without its soul.

Squeezed

If convicted of a capital offense,
offered my choice
of means of execution
I'd ask to be constricted
by a boa.

It is nice to be hugged.
Even nicer
to be hugged hard.
The boa's way at least begins
with a loving gesture.
It may get painful
toward the end.
Loving gestures
sometimes do that.

Epic Hope

Every human life's an epic poem
        some English teacher said.
Maybe so, I guess.
        Maybe so.

She didn't say that we are poems
        anyone would ever care to read.
Odysseys, Paradises Lost and Comedies Divine
        aren't found among the company I've kept.

We all need ruthless editors
        to erase prosaic stanzas,
to spin banal realities
        with titillating glosses.

I'd love someday to read the revised me
        printed on vellum,
Morocco bound,
        illustrated by Frida Kahlo
                or Paul Gaugin.

Missing My Muse

I've called and called, God knows,
sent e-mails. It all goes
unanswered by that sweetheart who once gave
me trenchant metaphor,
vibrant images galore
cast in lines to make the harshest critic rave.

My sultry-voiced songbird
has not bestowed one word
since Mardi Gras in Cozumel last year.
She gave me up for Lent,
then Pentecost, Advent,
Ramadan, Diwali, Yom Kippur.

I have this nagging dread
that some thing I did or said
makes me a thought she simply can't endure.
Does some celestial love affair
take all her time up there?
(How does a Muse amuse her paramour?)

Has some supernal shock
left *her* with writer's block,
so she, like me, can't generate a thing?
I sit here, stare and stew.
There's nothing I can do
to create lines that scintillate and sing.

But when she comes you'll see
poetic fluency.
My pen will race at record pace to write
a poem, or two or three
for all the world to see.
I'll take full credit in the copyright.

Notes

Rida, Rida, Ranka (p. 15). The title of the poem is the title of the Swedish children's song my grandmother sang. It means (roughly) "ride, ride a stick-horse." The Swedish hymn referred to is *Tryggare kan ingen vare*, known in English as *Children of the Heavenly Father*.

Heavens, It Was Tasty (p. 29). The title is adapted from Garrison Keillor's "commercials" for Powdermilk Biscuits on *A Prairie Home Companion*. The last line is stolen from T. S. Eliot, *The Love Song of J. Alfred Prufrock*. The Powdermilk Biscuit Bandman is Adam Grainger.

About the Author

Arnie Johanson is a Minnesota native, with degrees from the University of Minnesota and Yale University. He taught Philosophy at Minnesota State University, Moorhead for thirty-three years, retiring in 1999. He has been writing poetry ever since, through the inspiration of the Osher Lifelong Learning Institute at Duke University. He resides with his first and only wife, Alice, in Durham, NC and Minneapolis, MN. They have three adult children and four grandchildren.

www.ingramcontent.com/pod-product-compliance
Lightning Source LLC
Chambersburg PA
CBHW031437040426
42444CB00006B/858